A HOME for all Seasons

A Home for all Seasons

By Meg Lesser Roberts *and* Steven Roberts,
The Echo Design Group

Text by Brenda Cullerton

Photographs by Maura McEvoy

Harry N. Abrams, Inc., Publishers

Editor: Ruth Peltason
Designer: Ana Rogers

Library of Congress Cataloging-in-Publication Data

Roberts, Meg Lesser.
A home for all seasons / by Meg Lesser Roberts and Steven Roberts
; text by Brenda Cullerton ; photographs by Maura McEvoy.
p.   cm.
Includes bibliographical references and index.
ISBN 0–8109–3429–9 (hardcover)
1. Interior decoration.   I. Roberts, Steven, 1956–
II. Cullerton, Brenda.   III. McEvoy, Maura.   IV. Title.
NK2110.R59   1998
747—dc21   98–3500

 Harry N. Abrams, Inc.
100 Fifth Avenue
New York, N.Y. 10011
www.abramsbooks.com

Photograph Credits

All photographs by Maura McEvoy except for those on the following pages:
Patricia Heal: 28, 59; Meg Roberts: 32, 60

Interior Design Credits

JoAnn Barwick, Design Consultant: 29, 31; Kathleen Brenner: 58; Jeanne-Alia Desparmet-Hart:
20, 76, 104; Bruce Glickman, Washington, Conn.: 16, 18, 66–67, 70, 74, 84–85, 86, 96, 124,
125; Page Goolrick: 34–35, 37; Heidi M. Greene, Inc.: 25, 77, 101, 123; Regine Laverge,
Jardin Paradis, Washington, Conn.: 45; Amy Lesser: 102, 103; Suzy Taylor, ASID, Washington
Depot, Conn.: cover, 12–13, 23, 24; Becky Vizard, St. Joseph, LA: 100, 126; Kevin Walz: 22,
51, 87, 88, 89, 107, 111; Mark Zeff Consulting Group, Inc.: 50, 80, 106, 108, 117

contents

Echo's own chiffon scarves

preface

The year 1998 marks Echo's seventy-fifth anniversary. As the third generation of the company's founders, we are apparently beating the odds. And now, at this wonderful milestone in Echo's history, we find ourselves looking back. In 1923, our grandparents Edgar and Theresa Hyman incorporated on their wedding day what is today The Echo Design Group. Theresa adapted the brand name Echo from Edgar's initials, E. C. H., and added the "o" by creatively stealing the letter from "company," as in The Edgar C. Hyman Company. After having lost two jobs working for companies that went bankrupt, Edgar created a simple goal for himself: to make a living. He promised that on the third time out if he were going to lose a job he would do it on his own. Soon the company became more than a business. Make a fine product, he said, and offer a good value. Remember the golden rule: Do unto others as you would have them do unto you. Be honest. Be fair.

These philosophies have defined Echo ever since. No one who has visited Echo's offices could fail to see and feel that Echo remains a family-run business with Edgar's vision. Edgar and Theresa's only daughter, Dorothy Roberts (our mother, chairperson, and CEO), runs the business from an office that reveals much about the company. It is filled with a sense of warmth, openness, and good spirit. And it is literally decorated with what she considers her most valuable assets: photos of her growing family, the fourth generation.

As a married couple, like Edgar and Theresa, along with our sister, Lynn Roberts, and all the members of the Echo "family," we have a big responsibility—to carry Echo's spirit forward. To all of us it is a way of life. As the company expands and diversifies we continue to strive for innovation, integrity, quality, and a sense of style.

But why should a company famous for scarves, ties, and accessories do a book about the home? And why use the seasons as inspiration? The fact is, looking at life in terms of the seasons comes naturally for us at Echo. We've been in the fashion business for three-quarters of a century. And seasons are the lifeblood of fashion. They keep the creative juices flowing. More than simply changes in the weather, they mark changes of heart and mind, of spirit and style. Interpreting these subtle shifts of mood or attitude and bringing them to life through color, pattern, print, and texture is precisely what Echo is and has always been about.

Color. Pattern. Print. Texture. These four essential elements not only transform a piece of cloth into an accessory that helps define your own intensely personal sense of style, they also transform a house into a home—into a place that reflects who you really are. All of which explains why we at Echo now feel equally at ease, not to mention delighted, creating everything from bedding to superb quality wallpapers. For us, designing the details that help you express your individuality and style everywhere from the kitchen to the bedroom is no coincidence—it seems like yet another perfectly natural connection, a way of expanding upon the obvious.

In aligning ourselves with only the most prestigious names in the industry—names such as Revman, F. Schumacher, and C. R. Gibson—Echo also continues to build upon the traditions of quality and integrity that our parents and grandparents considered so vital to "success."

Enough said. As you begin visiting the homes in this book, we hope it will be apparent that the rooms chosen are ones that real people have come to love, not to mention to cook in, sleep in, and play with their kids in. In keeping with our own design aesthetic, these are rooms that have come into being gradually, over time. We believe this is what gives them a marvelous feeling of familiarity, of intimacy and warmth. Far from just nice places to visit, they are places that we would all enjoy living in.

MEG AND STEVEN ROBERTS

Imagine a child building a fort: the borrowed sheet, draped like a nomad's tent over a kitchen table, hangs just low enough to hide the mysterious, newborn space beneath. Furnished inside with pillows, a flashlight, and a few favorite toys, the fort isn't as flimsy as it seems. In the eyes and mind of a child, it's a blissfully safe and secret place. A place secure enough to withstand the force of imaginary hurricanes, storms at sea, even an invasion of aliens from outer space.

Eventually, the borrowed sheets give way to sturdier stuff: to plaster, bricks, wood, and steel. But the **fantasies** endure. "An anchor of being," "one of the greatest powers of integration for our thoughts, memories and dreams. . . ." This is how the French philosopher Gaston Bachelard talks about the houses we live in, both as children and as grown-ups. With fears of make-believe aliens replaced by grown-up realities, realities shaped by a need to be perpetually mobile, accessible, and up to speed, that "anchor of being" plays a more pivotal role in our lives than ever. It's why our houses, our homes, mean the world to us.

Stability, comfort, ease, order, beauty, style . . . these are all words we use to describe that ideal world and the feelings it evokes. Occasionally, however, those feelings run deeper. Think, for instance, of the moment one first sets foot into an unknown house. There's an almost gentle greediness in the way the eye wanders, focuses, absorbs, and how the hands long to touch things. Whether we're invited "in" through the pages of a book like this or by a neighbor down the street, once through the door, we all become explorers.

Propelled by an irresistible urge to see more, to travel yet further into the unknown, we roam through rooms and hallways, peeking into closets and hidden nooks and crannies. If we're lucky, the sense of discovery and of revelation, together with curiosity and delight, also inspires a renewed sense of our own potential.

"Ah! How come I didn't think of that?" or "Hey! What a great idea!" Transforming a narrow corridor or hallway into a picture gallery and choosing a deep shade of rose instead of the usual white, moving an antique table from indoors and down to a dock for a casual lobster dinner, alluding to the earth and sky with a surreal vision of painted clouds and pears on a porch ceiling—this is where the real joy of discovery lies. In suddenly stumbling upon the obvious and in making what might appear foreign or far-fetched feel instantly familiar, fresh.

Obviously, not everyone has the courage to paint clouds and pears on a porch ceiling. Because our homes mean the world to us, we take great pride in them. And with pride comes a degree of uncertainty, nervousness. Who, at one time or another, hasn't felt intimidated by a blank wall or an empty room waiting to be filled. "Where do I start?" "What if I make a mistake?" "What will people say?"

Decorating, creating "interior sensations" isn't nuclear physics. It's a form of thinking, even dreaming out loud. It's an explanation and an exploration of self. The more personal and detailed, the more generous one is with that explanation, the more compelling, not to mention honest, the results.

Following instinct and impulse are crucial in bringing that explanation to life. So, too, are color schemes, window treatments, fabrics, and wall coverings. But the process has to be more intimate and less clinical than, perhaps, these terms suggest. Because it really is what we associate and how we connect emotionally with everything, from the bare bones of a house to color, pattern, texture, and the tiniest objects that gives them dimension and depth. Of course, there are detours and dead ends along the way. But the pleasure, indeed the passion, is in the process, in the exploration and the effort.

People talk about the "art" of pulling all these various elements together. They say they owe it to inspiration. Inspiration, like art, can be hard to define. Sure, it comes in the form of memories, thoughts, dreams. It also comes in that instant when one first cajoles open a window after a long, cold winter and smells the green of newly mowed spring grass.

This is where "interior sensations" very often begin—with a primal response to the moods and moments of the seasons. With that quick-pulsed rowdiness of spring: the intoxicating scent and color of hyacinth and lilac, of daffodils and crocus. It's a reflex reaction—the sudden burst of hope and ambition that feels as fresh as the air itself. We clear out all the cobwebs and the clutter. We open all the windows.

Then comes the long light and pure elation of summer. Such intensity of pleasure. Hazy heat, drowsiness, and a longing to get lost in a vast expanse of blue-green water and sky. Summer is the season when simplicity is luxury; the season of sand-scrubbed cottons, clean white linens, and free-floating fabrics billowing like silk spinnakers in the wind.

Too soon, we find ourselves returning home to roots and to Keats's "mellow fruitfulness" of fall. Fall, for grown-ups, is a coming down to earth. It's the restoration of order, "the law of hoes and rakes." It's the sharpening of yellow pencils and piles of crimson and shiny brown leaves. Leaves as shiny and polished as the leather on a pair of Buster Brown shoes.

Fall offers a breathing space before the snow-stilled silence and uncovered distances of winter prompt us to shut and bolt the doors and to pull out books and soft, woven woolens. Winter is when we light a fire in the fireplace and settle in to wait, once again, for the pastel promises of spring. It's a time for seeking shelter, a time to embrace the comforts of home. As a symbol of the self—contained—, home assumes renewed significance throughout the holidays, a season in which children and grown-ups together decorate and embellish upon the nature of fantasies and dreams.

"The seasons seize the soul and the body," says the poet Charles Olson. Within the moods and moments, the structure and rhythm, of every season lies the ultimate explanation of who we are and who we wish to be. In a world where identities are now confirmed by numbers and machines seem to have more memory than we do, the seasons remind us of the joys of being human. Like the houses we inhabit, they manage not only to anchor but to move us: to comfort and to captivate. A Home for All Seasons celebrates that vital link between nature and emotion; a link that transforms plaster, bricks, wood, and steel into a place as blissfully safe and secure as the makeshift fortresses that dot the distant landscapes of childhood.

When,
nature's
optimism,
her resilience,
truly is
contagious

Spring

The triumph of the sun,
the squelch of mud and melting snow, rain,
restlessness, violets, a desire for blue,

Spring fever. It's that buzz of pleasure that comes with sitting on a stoop or opening the back door in the first warm days of May. The light lasts longer. The earth is showing vital signs of life. And heavy thoughts are shrugged off as lightly as a chiffon scarf that floats from a hook on a whitewashed wall. Nature's optimism, her resilience, truly is contagious.

With that sudden alertness, our eagerness to emerge from the snowy cocoons of winter, rooms that only months ago might have felt snug and cozy now feel small and overcrowded. We eliminate the clutter and let in light and air. Everything is scrubbed bright, made clean and painted in pale shades of baby pink and blue, fresh minted greens, and soft sunshine yellows. Like the innocence of gingham and rosebuds, spring's point of view is based on the sensation of brand-new beginnings.

It's a season that has the smell of the future in it. A smell as fresh and new as the starched linen sheets on a cloud-white bed, the spa-like vision of a white terrycloth

the glow of greenness, the glossy petals of a yellow tulip,
the shivering flight of a butterfly, the smell of fresh dirt,
lilacs

slipcover, even the metal insect legs of a skinny Jacobson chair. Whether primitive or

post-modern, Empire or Victorian, the mood is light, even whimsical.

There's nothing opaque or complicated about it. It's as transparent as curtains of thin cot-

ton voile caught up by sheer ribbon bows. Anything that threatens to confine or slow down

a renewed sense of motion and momentum is removed. Mirrors, frosted glass and crystal,

blond and painted woods, and wicker are other furnishings and decorative details that reit-

erate the season's "lightmotifs" and that emphasize a broadening of horizons — a surfeit of

space and air.

Bunches and bouquets of lilacs, lilies of the valley, forsythia and bluebells,

tulips drenched with dew . . . these are a few of the season's first and freshest picks. Set

out on windowsills and tables in sterling silver baby cups, cut glass, or a collector's favorite

McCoy vase, they more than fulfill the promises of new beginnings.

The lacquered checkerboard floor of pale green and creamy white in an attic bedroom

stirs and soothes reawakened senses of spring. So do fresh-picked floral prints, a

perennial favorite when it comes to taking our cue from nature and bringing the outdoors

in. Seen here in full bloom on a porch chaise, the print also alludes to the fact that

this is a room designed to function as part of both the inside and outside worlds.

Andr. Matthioli Comm.

POLYPODIVM.

FILIX MAS

FILIX FOEMINA.

THE GARDEN PRIMER BARBARA DAMROSCH

The Garden Room

THE GOLDEN AGE of AMERICAN GARDENS

Decorating with Flowers

Whether they are framed or tamed and growing in pots, the lacy fronds

of forest ferns glow with the greenness that is the essence of spring.

A feeling of the future

Newborn pink gingham, the homespun check coverlet, and dreamcatcher's

canopy (it's really mosquito netting) over a young girl's bed evoke all

the promise and spirit of innocence that are synonymous with spring.

The delicious confection of pale pastels in a kitchen breakfast nook seem almost good enough to eat—

and as fresh as the teatime selection of homemade fruit pies on a marble countertop that tempt the eye.

Tranquillity reigns, from the robin's egg blue walls of a luminously lit

living room (the barely there curtains are see-through cotton voile

gathered by sheer ribbon bows) and the stripes of a foyer chair to the

terrycloth slipcover on a Spanish settee in a divinely spare bathroom.

oh so serene
and almost spa-like

florabunda

Hyacinths, lilacs, daffodils, tiny crocus—the first flowers of spring

intoxicate with their heady perfume and dreamy colors.

A far-from-garden-variety floral chintz—the combination of Echo's "new" Nantucket comforter

and pillow and a vintage American quilt—make this painted sleigh bed a spring dream come true.

A collection of English creamware sitting pretty on a kitchen window ledge

together with walls as white as milk epitomize the idea of new beginnings.

scrubbed white

as the worlds turn

A vintage globe collection creates a decorative axis for this pristinely modern take on city dining. A restaurant supply company custom-made the table, and the chairs are reproduction Jacobson. (Fresh-cut grass in the centerpiece tray makes a witty allusion to distant country lawns.)

This might well be considered an homage to the architect Le Corbusier, a man who believed in the geometry of everyday objects as well as the impact of strong saturated color. The couch is his. The specific shade of the blue Barcelona chairs, however, was chosen based on the owner's childhood associations with her first Barbie car. Pride of place also goes to the meticulous arrangement of black-and-white photographs.

Convertible living,
top down, radio on,
an extravagance
of open space,
a feeling of uninhibited
ease

Summer

The slam of a screen door,
the fragrance of roses in hot sun,
tangerines and limes, the screech of a lifeguard's whistle,
deep sleep, a shower out-of-doors,

Translating the mood and the moment of summer into interior sensations is a breeze. It's convertible living. In every sense of the word. It's moving out-of-doors and onto front porches, beneath the beckoning eaves of Victorian verandas, into shady garden "rooms" created with a couch "slipcovered" with a favorite tablecloth. (Don't hesitate to put a sisal rug or oriental on the "floor," too.)

It's abandoning hard-and-fast rules and the rituals of routine in favor of a life as uncomplicated as the weather. It's taking liberties with time. (Summer is the only season when the jolt of an early morning alarm sets off a smile at the thought of catching waves and fish, not trains and carpools.) Free to drift, to dream, we adapt to nature's own exuberance. A sense of harmony prevails.

Heatwaves of brightly colored slipcovers in awning stripes and solids are set against bold buoyant whites and the mirage-like serenity of lake and ocean blues. Woods are raw or weathered by sea spray, wind, and rain. See-through curtains frame (versus block) an ever-present view, while cool fabrics like cotton, canvas, tickings, and

shade,
the snap of green beans, a glimmer of sea glass in sand,
a chorus of crickets, the creak of an old-fashioned rocking chair

vintage 1940s linens also define the essence of summer's nonchalance, its elegance and ease.

The fancy and the ornate, the fragile and the priceless seem somewhat heavy and out of place in summer's casual surroundings. Lightweight wickers and rattan, the open weave of metal garden furniture, the twiggy embrace of an Adirondack chair, and scrubbed pine farmer's tables. These are the contents of a summer world. A world in which nature puts her favorite possessions on temporary loan: a piece of polished driftwood, stones, and seashells. Together with fresh-cut flowers in a bright painted coffee can and the finds from local flea markets (unfussy, unframed sea and landscapes, the slightly chipped glaze of American pottery, mismatched china), these possessions more than satisfy our impulse to embellish.

It isn't a question of forgiving the rickety, the casual nicks and chips, or the quirks and eccentricities of a summerhouse. They are part of the relaxed charm, the attraction of a season whose allure lies in its transience and in our own capacity to make the most from the least.

turning life inside —out

The couch, draped with an old French tablecloth covered with morning glories

that doubles as a slipcover, and a cushiony hammock sum up the colorful

and casual ease of summer living. It is a season for rooms without walls,

rooms that feel as big and as spacious as the great outdoors.

la dolce vita

Set against an immensity of blue sky, rolling green lawns, and shade trees, the laid-back elegance

and the luxury of living, dining, perhaps even napping alfresco comes to life.

decorating is a form of dreaming out loud

It's an exploration and an explanation
of self. If that exploration occasionally
takes fantasy to new heights and
includes extraterrestrial visions of
floating clouds and ripe pears on a
garden room ceiling, so be it.

There is nothing elitist about the barefoot pleasures of a summerhouse.

Instead it's a place (and a frame of mind) where the parameters of possibilities and freedom are kept wide open.

open-door policy

the straight and the narrow

Stripes are not only precise, they can also be discreet or bold, purely casual and

deliciously sophisticated. Some are thin—the blue (and red) lines of traditional

ticking—and others come big and fat like beach cabanas and awnings.

It isn't just the idea of planting a profusion of roses on a living room couch that so distinctly suggests the atmosphere of summer. It's the antique wooden boat set to motor off in a bay window, the hand-painted geese decoys, even the red ticking pillow. All of it gives an informal feel to a paneled room that might otherwise have been construed as more austere. (The Austrian coffee table is antique cherry and big enough to put your feet up on.)

Sleeping with one's head in the clouds beneath a Carol Anthony landscape reflects the abundance

of summer light and suggests breezy thoughts of wind-filled spinnakers and mainsails.

bright (white) ideas

just add water

Tropical allusions abound in this wood-beamed country kitchen. The aqua window trims summon up visions of the Caribbean. An island feeling accentuated by the cool blue stripes of a cotton rug, the primitive Haitian paintings, and the splashes of pure, intense color seen in the collection of McCoy pottery.

climbing the walls

Trellised or latticed doors and windows and a splash of red roses trailing up the walls shed

an illuminating new light on conventional concepts of the old-fashioned (and somewhat

claustrophobic) linen closet. The rose-covered comforter and pillows repeat the theme.

A longing to get lost in a vast expanse of blue-green sea and sky.

the long days of summer

Imagine how a long, leisurely soak while reading a book in this bathing beauty (a white porcelain, claw-footed

tub) would take the heat off. The bucolic scene above the tub of a secluded lake in a forest and the vintage life

preserver hanging by the generous window are other watery allusions that befit the season. The sun-filled

mudroom offers an ongoing display of bits dug up in the garden: sparkly glass, smoothed-over stones.

Cocktails as the sun goes down. A sigh at the purple haze of dawn. And sitting down for a

lobster dinner at the water's edge. What better way to express the exuberance and elation of

summer. Placing a fine Early American table and Adirondack chairs on an empty dock

creates an instant outdoor dining room that feels as elegant as it is casual.

Romancing
the rough and the
rustic.
America's
pioneering
spirit

Fall

The scent of hickory and maple, an early morning mist spangled with sunlight, the crisp, clean taste of red apples and air,

Languorous ease, the indolence of summer is over. Invigorated by a change in the air and bracing ourselves for the season to come, there is a crispness, a decisiveness to our actions that perfectly mirrors the mood and moment of fall. We set off on brisk walks in the woods (versus lazy strolls along the beach). We unscrew screens and snap in storm windows. We sift and sort through cedar closets, attics, and storage spaces, pulling out everything from woolens and flannels to rubber boots and rain gear.

This surge of determined effort and activity is reminiscent of pioneers and frontier dwellers. Interiors romance these roots, too, with allusions to the rough and the rustic that can be found everywhere from hand-hooked rugs on terra-cotta floors, Indian baskets, faded Beacon blankets, and hutch tables to the wood plank floors and hand-hewn beams in a renovated country kitchen and the crafty imperfections of Early American ironware.

A western-style dining room, the discovery of an antler chandelier, a pony skin rug, or a log cabin quilt at an outdoor fair or flea market are all nostalgic souvenirs of lives lived in an age before remote control. A do-it-yourself age when rooms and the

the click of steel rings in a loose-leaf binder,
jack-o-lanterns,
the toastlike crackle of dried leaves and twigs, wet stones and moss

objects within them had to serve both purpose and passion. Happily, that same thriftiness of thought and design, of form and function, works as beautifully (and efficiently) today as it did yesterday.

As for color—science may have its own meticulous explanation for that mysterious alchemy that transforms green into shades of burnished gold (gold as warm as the polished copper pots hanging over a kitchen counter). But its magic never fails to move us. Taking our cues from nature, yet again, we bring the outdoors in, mixing yellow golds and crimson with bordeaux, chestnut browns, and muted mossy greens. A variety of tweeds, tartans, lumberjack plaids, and lush, faded florals mixed with paisleys are also synonymous with the mood of the season.

More food for thought? A voluptuous still life of deep purple eggplant, pumpkins, and painted gourds. Wooden bowls filled with ripe apples and pears. An homage to the abundance of the season's harvest, they taste as good as that first sip of beaujolais nouveau (a sip savored after carrying in the kindling for an old stone fireplace and slipping off a pair of heavy duty mud boots).

As one sets foot into an unknown house, there's an almost gentle greediness in the way the eye wanders, focuses, and absorbs, and how the hands long to reach out and touch things. The smallness of this book-lined room is no accident. The use of deep autumn olives on walls, the richly muted reds and oranges of a paisley throw and kilim upholstery, and the casual clutter of so many books and objects create a warmth and coziness that removes even the hint of a chill in the autumn air.

Forget technology for just a moment and the age of information on-line, this "reading room" vignette with books galore is a testament to the joys of old-fashioned page turning. The English library table is superb-quality reproduction, whereas the globes are authentic 17th century. The gift of a friend, they were lost then found wrapped in garbage bags in a basement storage room. The French still life was commissioned by the owner and is painted on tin.

The days of the real frontier may now belong solely to the realm of fiction, but the romance

lives on, especially in this civilized version of a western-style kitchen with its antler chandelier,

silver tea set, and pony-skin chairs. References to the less flamboyant but equally hardy spirit

of the New England settler is obvious in the Early American table set with ripe fall apples

and pears. The wooden banquette (softened with plump plaid and paisley pillows) transformed

what was once a vacant hallway into an invitingly comfortable sitting area.

o pioneer!

steps lively

An expert use of the fall color palette makes a marvelously unexpected decorative

statement on stairway risers. (An unexpected detail that strikes one as being more

calculated than coincidental is the antique beaded pear at the bottom of the banisters.)

the not so Wild West

An eclectic combination of fabrics (faux pony skin, needlepoint, wool plaid throws) looks right at home

when set against a backdrop of fieldstone—as at home as the African tribal masks, baskets,

and All-American rocker that so successfully marry the rough and the rustic with a touch of genuine ethnicity.

Roses on mochaccino wallpaper, the collection of green crockery, and majolica evoke the feeling of a Victorian period piece in this large but cozy dining room, while yellows mellowed by the late afternoon sun and burnished woods set a more minimalist mood for the roundtable dining scene.

A study in browns mixed with neutrals, toile, and plaids not only takes the edge off but unifies

the odd and intriguing angles of an attic bedroom, creating an impression of cozy spaciousness.

treehouse retreat

Sheltered beneath the garret eaves like a child's favorite treehouse, this bedroom, with its bird's nest prints and mix of plaids, stripes, paisleys, and even geometric patterns, proves there is harmony in contrast. Allusions to the nesting instinct assume a three-dimensional aspect with the twigs and berries seen beside the bed.

Just as the American colonial hutch was originally designed to suit practical and

aesthetic needs (it was an all-in-one storage space, bench, and occasional table),

the same might be said for islands in a country kitchen—ideal places

for cooking, eating, and chatting over a cup of coffee or a glass of wine.

like minds

A kitchen and a bath that share autumn traits: from the contrast of warm woods and whites

to the marble and antique hooked rugs on the floor.

A time
for taking cover,
for reveling
in the comfort
of man-made pleasures

Winter

Snowflakes as soft as a moth's wing,
featherbeds and eiderdowns,
the ice on tree branches that shimmers like sequins on silver,
a cord of wood stacked and split, the denseness of the dark,

Winter.

Think of that chilly moment of reckoning when toes tentatively edge their way off the bed, touch the floor, and pull back as if stung by the waves of a frigid sea. With trees bared to the bone and a landscape sketched in lines as stark as a charcoal drawing, winter is the season for seclusion, for pulling up the drawbridge like once-upon-a-time inhabitants of fairy-tale castles and surrendering to our instinct to retreat.

It's a time for taking cover. Literally and figuratively. For reveling in the warmth and comfort of man-made pleasures. An embroidered tapestry hung on the wall or in a doorway, a shawl draped invitingly over a plump down armchair, **overstuffed cushions,** and kilims and orientals flung one on top of another. Winter calls for a certain opulence of gesture. For a luxurious layering of fabrics, prints, and patterns. A needlepoint pillow resting on the red candy-stripe ticking of a cast-iron daybed, plaids mixed with Kashmir's royal paisleys, leather, damasks, velvets. All of these help fill in the season's blanks and soften harsh, cold edges.

The lucidity of winter's light, its astounding clarity and brightness, shines through the season's color palette: stark, lacquered whites combined with glossy blacks, subtle shades of gray, and a more than minimalist touch of deep forest greens, ocher, reds,

a snifter of brandy,
the smell of woodsmoke, the radiance of a pearl-white moon, icicle spears, catching jewels in the sun

and chocolate browns. The vision of a single, snow-white amaryllis, a far-from-shrinking African violet, even the exotic incongruity of a West Indian curry plant imply possibilities of warmth and inner growth as we snuggle in to read and reflect.

The classic lines and proportions of antique and modern furnishings are other man-made pleasures that befit the season. They fortify the spirit and lend a comforting bit of order and formality to rooms designed to shelter us from nature and the elements. Winter may also be the season we appreciate our possessions most. Collections of paintings, books, and cherished objects remind of us of the richness, the complexity of life's experience. They add depth to the coziness of small, self-contained rooms. (Rooms that glow with the light of fires in the hearth, glass and silk-shaded lamps, and the lustrous hand-rubbed patina of mahogany, oak, and honey-colored woods.)

Far from inanimate, these collections speak to us and others of the significance of connections. (After all, it is connections, hardly mere coincidence, that shape not just decor but destinies.) The provenance or origins of these collections, whether humble or grand, who made them, how and where we found them, and the simple fact we've chosen them gives them value.

light fantastic

Snow-white walls, ceilings, and slipcovers act as a perfect wintery foil

for the display of rich paisleys, orientals, and wood plank farmhouse floors.

The collection of intaglios, found in London, are 18th century.

The lamp that sheds a hearthlike glow on a painted French commode expresses much of the opulence

of gesture that winter calls for. As for the walls of the study, papered in Echo's own navy plaid,

they are covered with gold framed paintings, which range from the purely personal with

portraits of the owner's grandparents to fine art and flea market finds. Like the Toby mugs,

this room owes its spirit to the fact that it has evolved gradually over time.

Candlesticks like spears of ice crystals, a voluptuous French oil of ripe fruit

brought to life in the table centerpiece, white Wedgwood china, and the sheen

of bright golds (seen in the Dutch brass chandelier and ornate frames) conjures

up a winter banquet scene straight from an 18th-century novel. (The forest

green Echo wallpaper further enhances the feeling of seclusion and formality.)

cold comforts

The house as "an anchor of being," one of the greatest powers of integration

for our memories, thoughts, and dreams. Here a rigorous but reassuring sense of order

puts that theory into practice. Shades of dusty sage and neutrals and the texture

of soft velvets and tapestry complete the picture.

A fondess for burnished silvery tones, seen in the mercury glass lamp, and collections, such as silver jars, photographs, or even the assortment of ties on display, suggest the significance of connections. (Connections, after all, that shape not decor but destinies.)

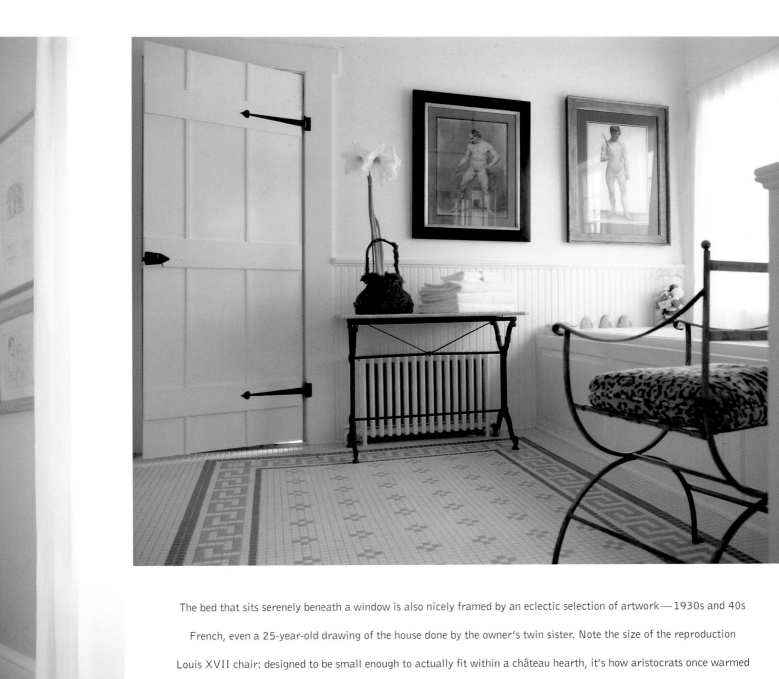

The bed that sits serenely beneath a window is also nicely framed by an eclectic selection of artwork—1930s and 40s

French, even a 25-year-old drawing of the house done by the owner's twin sister. Note the size of the reproduction

Louis XVII chair: designed to be small enough to actually fit within a château hearth, it's how aristocrats once warmed

their feet. There is a similar aristocratic feel to the formal bathroom, too, which is decidedly masculine in mood.

Like the winter landscape itself, this room is all cool restraint and symmetry. Tree bark browns, icy blues,

and eucalyptus greens—set against a blizzard of whites—make this interior as soothing as a silent snowfall.

perfectly composed

The kitchen is the heart of this house: in rooms cool and spare, as glittering

and clean as the thin skin of ice that coats tree branches in winter.

The marriage of candy-cane ticking stripes and needlepoint makes light of heavy metal on a cast-iron daybed. The pair of wooden feet set on a marble mantel (like a pedestal) elevate once-utilitarian objects into amusing art forms. It's not all in the details, however. The Anglo-Raj furnishings establish a wider context for the room in which the whole and the sum of its parts are equally compelling.

A childlike
.faith in
magic
and the
marvelous
Holiday

Tinfoil stars, letters to the North Pole, snowflakes cut from paper, spinning dreidels, frosted ferns on windowpanes,

Unraveling skeins of tiny white tree lights, polishing the family menorah, the eggshell-thin skin of glass ornaments—all shimmery shiny surfaces. What is it about the rituals of dressing up and decorating a home for the holidays that restores a childlike faith in the magic and the marvelous? Suddenly, the mundane, the everyday gives way to something more flamboyant and less restrained. As if to echo our own heightened sense of emotions and fantasy, the house is transformed.

The holidays offer all of us an invitation to imagine. Like sitting in a movie theater waiting for the lights to dim and the film to begin, it is an invitation to lose oneself in a moment that feels totally out of the ordinary, a moment that can be made to feel as dramatic as it is intimate and meaningful. Within this context, the house becomes a spectacular backdrop against which our own version of the holiday story and spirit unfolds.

Rich, sumptuous fabrics such as damasks, velvet, radiant silks, and tartans in jewel-toned colors of emerald, ruby, and sapphire enhance the magical impact of that story. Tradition, of course, plays an important role in the sense of occasion. But special personal effects can also add a dazzling twist of wit and whimsy. Consider, for instance, wrapping a garland around a bust like a boa and tying it up with bright gold ribbons or

the perfume of oranges and cloves, no school, angel hair, the brittle bright crunch of pine needles, New Year's Eve

embellishing a fir wreath with pears, pomegranates, and a big fat bow of red and chartreuse velvet scarfs.

As the only time of year when the power of both myth and belief happily coincide, a willingness to indulge the creative impulse is key. Tradition may call for liberal doses of red and green. Yet a window framed in evergreens set against French blue walls and a hot pink Toile de Jouy loveseat is equally festive and unexpected. (As unexpected as the idea of covering hatboxes in antique wallpapers and using them as giftboxes.)

Sometimes, the merest suggestion of the holiday spirit suffices: a fluted turquoise 1940s vase with a bouquet of green holly. Cherubs surveying a still-life of gold balls, a wagon-red amaryllis, and a Spode punch bowl. Far from trite clichés, it is the subtlety of these suggestions that adds elements of sparkle and surprise.

The anticipation and the pleasure of entertaining is as much a part of the holiday spirit as the decor. Toasting in the New Year at a table set for friends and family with a linen-lined tablecloth, lush, heavy cream-colored roses, sterling silver flatware, and fine white bone china makes the thought of future resolutions as easy to swallow as the deliciously icy bubbles of champagne in a perfect crystal goblet.

Whether the idea is extravagant and whimsical or blissfully simple

(holly in the perfect turquoise vase), the holidays are an open invitation to

embellish upon the intensely personal nature of fantasies and dreams.

rising
to the occasion

Here it means decking not just the halls but also the stairs

with boughs of evergreens and improvising a big, fat bow

from red and chartreuse velvet scarfs for the oversize wreath

hung on a French fruitwood armoire.

windows
of the soul

Many years ago, a family asked
friends to bring their menorahs
with them for a Chanukah party.
That idea has since become a ritual
for this annual gathering. Over time,
the number of friends and menorahs
has continued to multiply.

look homeward, angel

Gifts wrapped in antique wallpaper, ornament-trimmed hatboxes, and the stark elegance of a Spode punch bowl

are just a few holiday arrangements that help restore a childlike faith in the magic and the marvelous.

The tree was chopped down in a forest outside—a rustic gesture befitting the cottage-like feel of this country living room.

A liberal and luxurious mix of rich fabrics, yard dyes, needlepoint, toiles, and patterns adds a touch of warm sophistication.

holiday dressing

black tie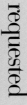

The use of heavy cream, gold, and black colors gives this dining room

a royal treatment, a sense of grandeur, which, together with the

Biedermeier-style chairs and 18th-century French mirror and

commode, sets the stage for an unforgettable New Year's celebration.

Acknowledgments

Many thanks to the remarkable team that was assembled for this project. Katie Matushak, Echo's home licensing manager, contributed invaluably from the conception of the book through to the last photograph. Her dedication and effort were immeasurable. Maura McEvoy's contributions went way beyond her obvious talent as a photographer. Her background as a stylist was very helpful, and her passion for the project was more than we could have hoped for. Brenda Cullerton provided the incredibly beautiful and intelligent text. She understood our vision perfectly, and then expressed it in a way that is quite literally poetry. Ana Rogers, the book's wonderful designer, took all the loose components of this project and brought them together with sensitivity and talent.

Amy Lesser, an architect and interior designer (and Meg's sister), performed brilliant pinch-hit styling, as did Bruce Glickman, an interior decorator and the owner of The Garden House in New Preston, Connecticut. We appreciate the tremendous creativity they brought to the shoots, as well as their willingness to roll up their sleeves and help with all sorts of myriad details.

We were assisted by so many people at Echo, but there are a few we must single out. Lynn Roberts (Steven's sister) was always ready to help style a shot, find the perfect prop, serve as a sounding board, or offer a valuable opinion. Hetty Easter valiantly held down the "Home" front and, along with Kim McAdam, coordinated our lives while we were on location. A special thank-you to Dorothy Roberts, our chairperson, and Charlie Williams, our co-president, for their usual guidance and for giving us their blessing.

We want to thank our wonderful licensing partners, C. R. Gibson, Revman Industries, and F. Schumacher & Co. for lending support and providing products when needed.

We are extremely grateful to all the people, most of them friends and neighbors, who so generously and graciously opened up their homes to us: Dr. Paul Adler and Monica Mahoney-Adler, JoAnn Barwick and Fred Berger, Andrew and Kathleen Brenner, Jim Caspi, Joan Caspi, Joseph Cicio, Michelle and Fred Daum, Glynnis Edmunds, Ginny Edwards and Tom Griffin, Bruce Glickman and Wilson Henley, Gael Hammer, Jeanne-Aelia and Steve Hart, Amy and David Kriss, Regine Laverge, Amy Lesser, Lynn and Mark, Brian Meehan, Peter and Abigail Murray, Larraine and Larry Nathanson, Pam and Todd, Joe Pintauro and Greg Therriault, Paul Scharfer, Suzy Taylor, and Amy and John Wickersham.

Many thanks to the following friends and retailers who provided props, time, and assistance: Aspetuck Gardens, Briggs House Antiques, Classic Cake Stands, Deirdre and Crosby Coughlin, Darien Reece Antiques, Dawn Hill Antiques, Decoration Day, Robin Fuchsberg, Garden House Antiques, J. Seitz and Co., Jonathan Peters, Terry Kemper, Kitchen Classics, Carolyn Klemm, The Old English Garden, Ray Baker Decorations, The Ritz, Shepaug Flower Farm, Susan Sirkman, The Trumpeter, Terri Windsor, and Mark Zeff.

We must also thank Lisa Finch, who not only managed our household during the busiest times of shooting, but lent a helpful hand to the project in countless ways.

And of course a very special thank-you to our editor, Ruth Peltason, for taking that first meeting, and for her expertise and guidance through every phase thereafter.

Last, we thank our children, Sam, Charlie, and Lily, for brightening our home in all seasons.

MEG LESSER ROBERTS AND STEVEN ROBERTS